P9-CRZ-098
Mullin

Stories
For Young
Americans

William Barret Travis

"Victory or Death!"

by Jean Flynn

EAKIN PRESS ★ AUSTIN, TEXAS

OTHER BOOKS BY THE AUTHOR

- ★ Jim Bowie
  A Texas Legend
- ★ Stephen F. Austin
  The Father of Texas

Art by G. E. Mullan

Published in the United States of America
By Eakin Press, P.O. Box 23066, Austin, Texas 78735

Stories For Young Americans Series

ISBN 0-89015-348-5 HB
1-57168-643-6 PB

In Memory
of My Mother

Portrait of Colonel Travis at the Alamo by H. P. McArdle
—Courtesy Daughters of the Republic of Texas

TABLE OF CONTENTS

I

THE PRANKSTER

"What have we here?" Mark Travis asked. No one was near the cow pen gate to answer him. Mark stepped closer to the basket tied to the gate. "Well, I'll be loco if'n it isn't a babe!" He grabbed the child and ran back to the house forgetting his chores.

Jemima heard her husband calling to her. She knew by the sound of his voice that he was excited. Before she could finish drying her hands on her apron, Mark handed the baby to her.

"Look what I found in a basket tied to the bar of the gate!" he said.

His wife was speechless. They took the baby inside their small cabin. Carefully Jemima unwrapped the crying child. "Hush, little one," she whispered and gently cradled the baby boy on her shoulder.

"We can't call him little one for long," Mark shook his head curiously. "Wonder who would abandon such a small babe?"

"Let's call him Bar after the place he was found," Jemima suggested. "Bar, William Bar. That's what we will call him."

They never found his parents. Some people said Indians had left the child because they didn't want him. Some said the child's mother had died and the father couldn't care for him. Some people said the foundling later changed his name to William Barret. And so the legend of the foundling grew.

Mark and Jemima Travis did find a child. They

did adopt him and raise him as their own. But he was *not* William Barret Travis who came to Texas. William Barret Travis, the Texas hero, made a legend of his own.

The Travis family can be traced in American history to 1624. The first family came from England to settle at Jamestown. They were close friends with the family of William Barret. Before the American Revolution the two families were wealthy landowners. They moved to James City County which was later known as Surrey County, Virginia.

Both families were leaders in the county. They were in the same social circles. They had the same wealthy standing in the community. For generations they remained in the same area. Many of the Travis family married into the Barret family. Children of the two families were named after both in first names.

Barret Travis, William Barret Travis' grandfather, lived in Virginia before moving to South Carolina. When he died, he left his estate to be divided among his sons and sons-in-law. During that time (1800s), daughters could not inherit land or money according to state law. The only way a daughter could inherit her share of an estate was if her husband had died.

Mark Travis inherited $374.83 when his father, Barret Travis, died. Mark, who was born in Cambridge, Edgefield County, South Carolina, on September 6, 1783, used his inheritance to establish himself as a landowner.

When he was twenty-five years old, he chose his bride. He and Jemima Stallworth were married on January 1, 1808. Like Mark, Jemima came from strong settlers. She was of Irish descent.

Their first-born, a boy, was a combination of the two parents. He had his father's ruddy face and long body. He had his mother's reddish hair and sensitive nature. William Barret Travis was born on August 1, 1809, at Red Bank Church, South Carolina. He was the first of ten or eleven children born to Mark and Jemima. The records are not clear on all of the children. But there is no doubt about William Barret Travis who was to give his life for Texas.

During the first nine years of his life, the young Travis formed a friendship with James Butler Bonham. The friendship was to last their short lifetimes. The strong bond between them brought them together at the Alamo.

James Butler Bonham was two years older than Travis. That did not bother them. Jim lived on his father's plantation about five miles northwest of Travis, whom he called Buck. They went to the same field school.

Most of the children did not attend the one-room school regularly. Jim and Buck did. Except when they slipped off to go horseback riding. They could not resist exploring. Both were adventurous and impetuous. They did not always think through what they were doing. They often acted quickly. They often found themselves in trouble.

Their teacher knew that when one was missing, the other one would be too. Sometimes the two boys slipped away to hunt. At other times they could be found fishing. The stories about hostile Indians did not worry them.

From an early age, they had owned their own horses. Both the Travis and the Bonham families owned large plantations. Slaves worked for their fathers. The boys did not have to help with the work on the plantations. They had plenty of time to get into mischief.

They often played tricks on the other children who attended the same school. Not all children had horses to ride to school. Some walked several miles each day. The trails were rough through tall trees and brushy land that had not been cleared for farming. It was spooky to walk through at the end of the day.

Buck and Jim grew tired of fishing one day when they had skipped school. The fish weren't biting. They hadn't seen any wild animals to hunt down. Their active minds began to plan. By midafternoon they had worked out a plan to entertain themselves.

They rode their horses to one of the wooded trails where several children walked to and from school. The spring afternoon was quiet. Birds hopped from tree to bush, snapping up insects. Sounds from surrounding farms occasionally floated through the thicket. As the sun sank deeper into the west, long dark shadows fell across the trail.

Buck and Jim sat still on their horses. The horses grazed steadily on new spring grass. They heard the children coming before they saw them. The children laughed and talked while they walked along the trail. Some of them carried books. The smaller ones were almost running to keep up with the long strides of the older children.

Buck and Jim stayed still while the children passed where they were hiding. They waited until they could barely hear their voices in the distance. With a nod to each other they began to yell, "Injuns! Injuns!"

Putting their heels to the horses flanks, they

took off in a hard run whooping like Indians. At the first scare, the children's screams echoed through the thicket. Mischievous smiles covered the prankster's mouths while they whooped and hollered.

After a short distance, they stopped to laugh at the scare they had given the children. They were bent almost double in laughter and tears were running down their flushed cheeks. They could not talk for laughing.

Suddenly Jim fell off of his horse. Before Buck could ask what had happened, he felt a swat with a branch of a tree. He grabbed the horse's mane to keep from falling. His attacker grabbed the horse's reins.

The oldest girl in the group of children had waited for them. She had knocked Jim off his horse and was now after Buck. He tried to move his horse but she wouldn't let go of the reins. A tug of war began. Buck lost. One swift swat with a green tree branch and he landed on his backside on the hard trail.

Both boys were still trying to get their breaths back when the girl swatted the horses. The horses took off up the trail toward the schoolhouse. They didn't seem to heed the boys' yelling, "Ho there! Whoa now!"

As they ran after the horses, they heard the girl yelling at them, "Maybe you better get more book learnin'. No smart Injun's goin' to let you know he's comin'."

They skirted around the girl at school for weeks. They were glad when her family moved on westward to new territory.

"I hope she runs into real Injuns," Jim whispered to Buck when the teacher told the students where the family had gone.

"Poor Injuns," Buck whispered back and rubbed his backside.

But Buck did not always play at school. He was a quick learner. He was fast in arithmetic and he liked to read. From an early age he read classical literature. Robin Hood was one of his favorite characters.

Not all of his heroes were in the stories that he read. South Carolina had its own "Robin Hood." Francis Marion was the "Robin Hood" of the American Revolution in South Carolina. He did not live in the Piedmont area of the state where the Travis family lived. But word of his work was passed among all South Carolinians even though at the time he was unknown to the rest of the country.

Francis Marion was born on a plantation in Berkeley County, South Carolina, in 1732. He learned fighting strategy in the Cherokee wars. People looked upon him as being the most brilliant guerrilla leader in the Revolution. And like the age-old Robin Hood of literature, he wanted to help his people.

Marion was a small man. He was dark and courageous. He was very independent. Many people loved him and many people hated him. He was beloved by his friends and his brigade. He was equally hated by his enemies.

Men looked upon him with great confidence in his leadership ability. Even his enemies respected him as a leader although they feared him. He was always at the head of his forces when he went into battle. He soon earned the name "Swamp Fox" because he could slip through the damp lowlands and make his kill as cunningly as a fox. He and his men slipped quietly out of thickets to attack their enemies and do as much damage as possible. And just as quietly and quickly, they disappeared into the dense jungle-like forest.

William Barret listened to the stories about the man who had died in 1795, years before he was born. He pretended he was with "Swamp Fox" on raids against the British. He slept beside the leader on the ground. He shared food with "Swamp Fox" when they cooked wild game over low fires. He relived the time that "Swamp Fox" and his men placed blankets across bridges to muffle the sounds of their horses' hooves. They stealthily sneaked up on the British and attacked without warning. In his daydreams, "Swamp Fox" always patted him on the back for being so brave.

Each time Travis put on a cap to protect his ears from the cold, he pictured himself as one of Marion's Brigade. The brigade had no uniforms. The only thing they had in common was a brown leather cap. Their motto was burned across the front of the cap for all to see — "Victory or Death."

Travis entertained himself for hours in his game of pretense. His well-kept clothing became rags on his small body. He scrounged for food where he thought hungry soldiers would look. His hunting gun leaned against his shoulder, ready for battle. When "Swamp Fox" gave him an order, he stood tall and saluted his leader.

His straight fingers gently touched the words burned on his cap. When the young boy, William Barret Travis, pretended bravery as "Swamp Fox's" comrade, he did not know that one day he would not pretend. When he touched the words burned on his cap, he could not have dreamed that he too would be remembered for the words "Victory or Death!"

II

THE SERIOUS STUDENT

"Why can't I stay here with Jim?" the nine-year-old Buck asked his father.

"Because we have sold our plantation here and are moving to Alabama Territory." Mark Travis tried to be patient with his oldest son. "We will have a better chance to buy more land, better land."

"Then can Jim come with us?" Tears began to fill Buck's eyes when he looked at the loaded wagons.

"You'll be seeing Jim Bonham again, never fret," Mark comforted his son.

Mark Travis had sold his plantation in the foothills of South Carolina. The Travis family was migrating westward toward new country. The land toward the Gulf Coast country was rich and fertile.

Mark settled his family on a farm near Sparta in Conecuh County, Alabama. William Barret was to continue to grow up in the middle of history-making events. In South Carolina he had lived in the shadow of the legends which grew around "Swamp Fox." When his family moved to Alabama in 1818, he heard tales of the heroes of the Creek War.

From the days of the American Revolution men of venturesome natures had made their homes among the Creek Indians in Alabama Territory. The adventurous white settlers had chosen lands that suited their fancy and bought directly from the Indians. Most of the time they traded axes and other farm implements for the land.

As the United States purchased and conquered more and more lands, the Indians grew fearful. The white settlers were beginning to take over the Indians' ancestral lands. The great Shawnee war chief Tecumseh tried to get the tribes to unite and drive the American settlers from the land. The Tuckabatchee leader Big Warrior led the peace group of the Indian nation. He would not agree to war. Choctaw Chief Pushmataha refused to listen to Tecumseh's plea for war.

In July, 1813, Colonel James Caller led an American attack on a group of Creek Indians at Burnt Corn Creek. The Americans won the first attack. The Indians withdrew and then counterattacked. The Americans scattered. The Indians redoubled their preparations for war. They scorned the Americans for being weak people.

At noon on August 30, 1813, the Indians, led by High Head Jim, swept into Fort Mims. They massacred most of the people and took the rest prisoners. The Indians were very cruel because many of those present at Fort Mims were part-Indian and considered traitors to their tribes. The records were not clear but some said about 553 men, women, and children were massacred.

Feeling very confident after the bloody massacre at Fort Mims, the Indians soon attacked Leslie's Station. Fourteen whites and about 125 friendly Indians were besieged for many days. One of the Indians was able to slip away from the fort. Legend spread that the Indian killed a large pig and used the skin as a disguise. While the captives of the station bombarded the Indians with fire, the "pig" crawled over dead bodies to escape into the dark.

An Indian messenger did reach Andrew Jackson. Jackson was already gathering Tennessee volunteers. He marched at once to aid the people at Leslie's Station. As they rode through communities, their voices reverberated in the trees and bounced off the walls of settlers' cabins, "Remember Fort Mims!"

The Americans marched on, winning battles as they went further south. Finally Jackson and his men met the Indians on March 27, 1814, in the largest and worst battle of the Creek War. The Battle of Horseshoe Bend ended the power of the great Creek Confederacy. The battle brought fame to Andrew Jackson.

The battle also brought attention to Davy Crockett and Sam Houston. They were with Andrew Jackson in the Creek War. Sam Houston had been wounded three times but he fought until the end of the war. An eager nine-year-old listener, William Barret Travis, did not know that he would some day fight side by side with his heroes. Neither did he imagine the reverberating sounds of "Remember Fort Mims" turning to an agonized echo of "Remember the Alamo!"

After the Treaty of Fort Jackson on August 8, 1814, the Creek Indians were forced to cede their lands to the United States. Vast tracks of rich land with ample river outlets for marketing were made available to the white settlers.

Mark Travis made a wise investment in 1818 when he migrated to Alabama Territory. He purchased 82.51 acres of land. Each acre cost $1.25. Mark prospered on his new farm. Soon he owned several hundred acres of land. The farm was well stocked with cattle. He owned a dozen or more slaves.

William Barret, along with his brothers and sisters, attended another field school which rapidly grew in size. The centrally located, one-room school drew students for miles around. The teacher quickly recognized Travis' ability and eagerness to learn. As he grew older, Travis read more and more classical literature.

Alabama was a rapidly growing country. The territory was admitted to statehood in 1819 because of its increase in population. Its admission to statehood brought many cultural and economic advancements. The slave population increased with the development of large plantations. Cotton growing became the major source of income.

Prosperity in farming brought other changes. Newspapers were established. The settlers were a part of a growing country, and they wanted to be informed about their government. Schools were founded. The one-teacher, neighborhood schools were no longer teaching all that the students needed to learn.

William Barret attended neighborhood schools with his brothers and sisters. Because of his ability and eagerness to learn, he was encouraged to go to a higher level of learning.

For a time he was enrolled in the Academy of Professor McCurdy in Monroe County. He is considered the most famous graduate of Sparta Academy. Evergreen Academy in Conecuh County also boasts of his attending there.

He was always interested in precise written words as well as the rhythms of oral expression. Both his writing ability and speaking ability were valuable to him later. He remained a lover of classical literature.

Judge James Dellett of Claiborne recognized William Barret's talent. Dellett was one of the best criminal lawyers in the state of Alabama. He befriended William Barret and tutored him in the complexities of the law. Dellett's tutoring was a substitute for a college education.

Dellett was also a politician. He was the first speaker of the House of Representatives. He set a good example for Travis to follow. He tutored him in more than law.

In April, 1825, when Travis was only sixteen years old, Dellett asked him to assist him in an elaborate ball for a visiting dignitary. The French general, Marquis de Lafayette, was to visit Claiborne which was the principal town in the county.

Travis accepted his responsibility gladly. He worked for days planning the elaborate ball. People for many miles around were invited. He made arrangements for the catering of the food to be served. He engaged a band to furnish the music.

Travis was also invited to attend the ball. He loved to dress elegantly. Dellett smiled his approval when he saw the young man in his bright red pantaloons. Travis had already grown most of his six feet plus height. He was a handsome blue-eyed, reddish haired young man. He was dramatic in his flashy dress clothes.

Dellett, who was a colorful speaker and a good actor himself, realized that Travis was patterning himself after his older tutor. He saw an obstinate set to his young friend's chin. He had heard Travis' outspoken opinions and knew the young man would go far in his profession.

By the time Travis was nineteen, he was teaching school as well as studying law. He was admitted to the bar in Monroeville before his twentieth birthday. He set up a law practice in Claiborne and Clarksville. Immediately his law practice prospered.

On October 26, 1828, Travis married Rosanna E. Cato. Rosanna was a former student of Travis. She was the beautiful daughter of a well-to-do farmer in Monroe County. Travis believed at that moment that his happiness was complete. His law practice was successful. His home was filled with his love for his beautiful wife.

The community respected the young, prosperous lawyer. He knew that he was accepted in the community when he was installed in the Alabama Lodge of the Masonic Order of Claiborne in August, 1829.

August of 1829 was a happy month for Travis. On August 8th, his son Charles Edward was born. Travis had been worried about Rosanna. She had become silent near the time for their child to be born. He believed that after his son's birth that she would regain her happy, beautiful spirit.

Rosanna loved their son but she was never the same after Charles Edward's birth. Travis threw himself into his work, taking on more and more responsibilities.

On January 3, 1830, he was awarded a commission as adjutant of the Twenty-Sixth Regiment, Eighth Brigade, Fourth Division of the Alabama Militia. He was a successful military man. He gained valuable experience in clerical duties and other correspondence.

By 1831 Travis was a very unhappy man. He was associated with the minority political party.

The minority party lost every issue to which it was opposed. The party fought against and lost to the group which wanted to move the county seat from Clarksville to a more central location in Clark County.

His marriage to Rosanna was in trouble. They had drifted apart after Charles Edward's birth. Rosanna was expecting another child. She too was unhappy with their marriage.

Travis read with interest the reports of settlers going to Texas. Foreigners were invited to settle in Texas and live ten years free of taxes and duties. Each family received a league of land, 4,428 acres, for approximately thirty dollars. In return the settlers had to take an oath of allegiance to Mexico, bring a letter of recommendation from their last place of residence, and promise to be a Catholic. After weeks of gathering information, Travis decided that Stephen F. Austin's colony was the place to go. Austin was empresario for three hundred families.

The decision to leave weighed heavily upon Travis' mind. He loved his son and did not want to leave him. He thought about the law practice he would leave behind. The decision was finally made quickly.

Travis went to Andalusia, Alabama, to conduct some legal business for a client. He tied his horse to the rail in front of the law office where he was visiting. The business took longer than he had planned. Although dusk was approaching, several men stood across the street waiting for him to mount his horse. Travis looked from the smiles on their faces back to the horse. Someone had cut off his horse's tail.

"I'll never live again in a state where such acts are committed!" he vowed. He mounted his tailless horse and with as much dignity as he could muster, rode past his political enemies.

And so early in 1831, William Barret Travis began his trip to Texas. He took only his black slave Ben. He left behind the many advancements created by the Industrial Revolution. The steam press, railway development, the comforts of a civilized society were all things of the past for Travis. He left behind his pregnant wife and two-year-old son.

He simply joined the throng of men who were moving to Texas. Some of the men were moving westward to begin a new life with the promise of free land. Some were challenged by a wild, untamed country that offered excitement and adventure. Some saw Texas as an escape from things they did not want to face. Some saw the move west as an opportunity to prove their worth.

Perhaps Travis was a combination of all of those reasons for moving to Texas. He was smart enough to know there would be a demand for lawyers. He was adventurous enough to want the excitement of the wild, untamed country. And he was unhappy enough to want to escape from things he could not change.

With a lighter heart than he had felt in months, Travis began the long journey to Texas. Texas, where all of the excitement of great adventures lay ahead of him. He did not feel the premonition of fear for what was to come.

He had grown up with the stories of heroes in the country where he lived. "Swamp Fox," Andrew Jackson, Sam Houston, and Davy Crockett were all wrapped up in the frame of William Barret Travis, who would make a legend far greater than he had ever dreamed.

III

THE GROWN PRANKSTER

March 2, 1831, found Travis in Anahuac, the chief Texas port on Galveston Bay. Anahuac was an established city. It was well laid out with shops and a plaza. A Mexican garrison was established there so the city included the soldiers and their families.

Travis was right in assuming the open country would welcome lawyers. He immediately established a lasting friendship with Patrick C. Jack, another young lawyer.

Travis and Jack met while they were boarding at the Hardins, the owners of an inn. The Hardins were hospitable people and made the young men welcome. They decided to open a law office in partnership. They opened their law office in the garrison outpost. They began immediately to learn the Spanish language and to study Mexican law for the Mexican population far outnumbered the Americans in Anahuac.

Travis and Jack were similar in nature. Both were capable leaders with similar backgrounds. Both were very patriotic. They didn't mind the long hours they studied the Mexican language and laws. Both were quick learners.

They soon formed a friendship with another young lawyer, R. M. Williamson. Williamson was known as "Three-Legged Willie." An illness at the age of fifteen kept him confined to a bed for two years. His right leg was permanently drawn back at the knee. A wooden leg was attached at the bend of the knee. He had trousers made with three legs and wore his shoe on the protruding foot.

He was a brilliant lawyer. He had begun practicing law in Georgia when he was only nineteen. He, like Travis, read classical literature. "Three-Legged Willie's" idol was the British poet Byron. Byron too had been a cripple but was handsome and brilliant.

"Three-Legged Willie" often entertained the young men. He was sociable. He didn't mind his nickname because it was the custom of the times to call people by nicknames. He was a good storyteller and banjo player. He published *The Texas Gazette,* which often included English poets' verse.

Travis, Jack, and Williamson were kindred souls. They were conspicuous wherever they went. Willie, with his three-legged pants, Jack in his long-tailed black coat, and Travis in his red pantaloons and white hat always attracted attention. They knew how to drink, gamble, and frolic. They also knew how to be businesslike. They spent many hours working, thinking, and planning.

In May, 1831, Travis applied for a "headright" in Stephen F. Austin's colony. He gave his age as twenty-two and listed himself as an unmarried lawyer. He asked for one-fourth league of land. Although he was admitted into Austin's colony at Anahuac, his grant was never registered. He later (in 1835) received a league of land in Milam's colony.

The Mexican Law of April 6, 1830, was the beginning of the end of Mexican rule over Texas. Travis was well aware of the law when he requested his land in 1831. The law restricted the westward movement from the United States to Texas. The Mexicans had become afraid that they had been too liberal in giving away land. The American settlers were outnumbering the Mexicans in many settlements. The Mexicans became suspicious and grew afraid of a settlers' rebellion against their rule.

Travis wasted no time in establishing the legality of his presence in Texas. He did not appeal to John Davis Bradburn, the newly appointed commander of the military garrison at Anahuac. Bradburn was trying to enforce the immigration laws. Had Travis gone to him before securing some legal protection there, he would have clashed with the military commander before he did.

Travis had a strong dislike for Mexican authority. The colony grants were suspended although they had not been completed according to agreement. The settlers had had to produce a letter of recommendation before they were accepted into a colony. Yet, the Mexicans were now occupying the colonies with convict soldiers.

In addition to those outrageous acts, the Mexicans had established custom houses on the Texas coast. Prior to the Law of 1830, no duties had been collected on importation.

Execution of the law had been given to General Manuel de Mier y Terán. Terán had suggested most of the law. He placed about 1,300 Mexican soldiers in the towns and villages of the province. He established a new post at Anahuac. At the same time custom houses were set up and a war vessel patrolled the coast.

Many of the men who were sent to command the posts were capable and honest men. They won the respect of the colonists. Two of them, neither Mexican, became well-known for their lack of ability and judgment in dealing with the Texans. George

Fisher, a Serbian adventurer, was appointed collector of customs for the port of Galveston. John Davis Bradburn, a native of Kentucky, was appointed military commandant at Anahuac.

Davis had been in the mercantile business with his brother in Mississippi. Both became involved in an argument over slaves and were put in jail. They planned an escape from the jail. Davis' brother drowned in the attempt but Davis managed to flee to Mexico. He enlisted in the military and gradually worked his way into becoming the commander of the forces at Anahuac.

Terán instructed Davis to move cautiously and to use local citizens to help build the garrison. He was to assure the inhabitants of Anahuac that they could act through him to gain title to their lands. He was to make every effort to establish good relationships with the colonists.

Bradburn was a bully. He immediately aroused the anger of the Texans with his arrogance. He blocked land titles for the settlers. He used slave labor without pay and treated all slaves poorly.

Travis disliked the man from the moment he met him. He and Jack set out to annoy Bradburn. They played pranks and practical jokes on Bradburn at every opportunity. The pranks always made Bradburn look ridiculous. Bradburn vowed to get even.

His chance to even the score with Travis and Jack came in 1832. Some prominent citizens, merchants, and lawyers met to discuss the payment of certain duties. They formed a company to resist payment of fees that they felt were unfair. They pretended the group was organizing against Indians. Patrick Jack was elected captain of the group.

Bradburn heard about the group and who was

captain. He had Jack arrested. Jack was held prisoner on a schooner in the bay. Dr. N. S. Labadie and "Three-Legged Willie" went to see Bradburn after two previous visits had failed.

Willie became very excited, cursed Bradburn, and told him, "Both of us will shed blood this day if Jack is not released!"

Jack came ashore around three o'clock. Americans lined up on either side of the riverbank and cheered as he came through. Bradburn's face was fiery red with anger. Jack's freedom lasted a very short time. But the next time he was imprisoned, Travis was his roommate.

Bradburn circulated false rumors that all slaves had been freed. Two runaway slaves came to him for protection. The owner, William Logan, demanded that Bradburn return the slaves to him. Bradburn demanded proof of ownership before he would release them to Logan.

When Logan returned with his receipt of purchase, Bradburn said, "The slaves have enlisted in the Mexian army. I must protect them under my country's flag."

Logan went to Travis and Jack for legal assistance. Travis was unable to get the slaves released by legal methods so he plotted to trick Bradburn. Travis started a rumor that a magistrate and one hundred armed men were marching to Anahuac to rescue the two slaves held by Bradburn.

Bradburn became afraid that the rumor was true. Then he received two letters telling him that the volunteers were coming for the slaves. He sent out scouts, ordered the garrison to parade, and kept the garrison under guard all night.

When nothing happened, he became suspicious.

He ordered the person who delivered the message to be brought to him at once.

The man who delivered the letters to Bradburn remained stonefaced when he answered Bradburn's question. "No, I didn't see the messenger clearly. His face was shadowed, but he was a tall man, wrapped in a big cloak. He just told me to get them to you."

The description fit Jim Bowie. Bradburn now knew who was behind the rumor. Bowie was a friend of Travis. Someone had dressed like the big man and delivered the message. He sent a file of thirteen officers to Travis' office to arrest him. Jack went with Travis to see what the charges were.

Jack and Bradburn already had hard feelings between them. Neither liked the other man. They quickly got into an argument. Harsh words were said by both Travis and Jack. Bradburn had the military power behind his anger so he had both men put in jail.

Colonel James Morgan, one of the principal merchants of Anahuac, offered to put up everything he owned as bail if Bradburn would release the two men. Bradburn refused. Travis and Jack were kept in close confinement. They could not speak to anyone. Their close friends were turned away from the garrison.

Travis and Jack were given stale bread and beans to eat. Lieutenant Juan Cortina and Colonel James Morgan began to slip food to them. Hannah, Morgan's slave girl, kept them in clean clothes. After about two weeks in prison, the officer of the day found a letter in the bundle of clothes that implied a prison break.

Bradburn acted at once. His prisoners were not going to escape. They had made a fool of him too many times. This was his chance to get even with Travis and Jack. He put all carpenters and masons to work on a new fort. He built the fort about one-half mile south of Anahuac.

When the fortification was complete, the prisoners were moved. An attachment of armed soldiers flanked the prisoners on both sides as they marched from the old garrison to the new prison. The prisoners' friends stood inside the fences of their yards and waved to Travis and Jack. Jack, dressed in his long-tailed black coat, waved back. Travis, flashy in his white hat, red pantaloons and black boots, bowed to his audience with great flourish. Their friends tried to assure them with gestures that help was on the way. They feared for Travis' and Jack's lives.

Bradburn knew the Texans were angry. He threatened to send his prisoners to Matamoros to be tried for treason and rebellion. Then he threatened to send them to Veracruz to be tried by military court.

William A. Jack, Patrick's brother and a lawyer in San Felipe de Austin, rushed to Anahuac. He told Bradburn, "You are acting in an illegal way. You must release the prisoners at once."

"You be out of Anahuac in fifteen minutes or I'll put you in the calaboose with them!" stormed an angry Bradburn.

William Jack left. He felt he could be of greater use to them free than in jail with them. He returned to San Felipe de Austin to raise a volunteer group to attack the fort at Anahuac.

The colonists were already angry about too many injustices. They acted quickly. They captured some Mexican guards and offered to exchange them for Travis and Jack. Bradburn agreed. He demanded that his men be released first. When the Mexican guards were freed, Bradburn refused to release Travis and Jack. He ordered that Travis and Jack be tied down and horsewhipped.

The Texans were outraged. Travis and Jack did not stand a chance unless they acted quickly. They had no hope of overthrowing the new fort without a cannon. The only cannon was at Brazoria on the Brazos River, a hundred miles to the west.

The quickest way to get the cannon from Brazoria to Anahuac was by boat. A schooner was lying at mooring on the Brazos River. When the men from Anahuac arrived at Brazoria, the captain of the schooner was not there. The boat's mate offered to help the Texans operate the vessel if he did not have to fight.

They loaded the cannon on the schooner and set out. There was one major problem. The schooner had to pass the Mexican garrison at Velasco, twenty-five miles downstream. The fort at Velasco was circular. It was built of logs and sand and surrounded by a stockade. The fort also had a large cannon.

The Texans centered their attention on the cannon. They had to keep anyone from firing it until the ship passed the fort. The high wall offered protection from the Mexicans' fire if they could slip next to it without being heard. They slipped ashore and moved toward the fort.

The men had to work in total silence so the Mexicans would not be warned of their attack. Their guns were unloaded to prevent accidental firing. Everyone but one man followed instructions.

Around midnight on June 25, 1832, Edward Robinson, a volunteer from Brazoria, let out a yell and fired at the fort. He was inexperienced, overzealous, and very excited. His shot revealed the position of the Texans. The Mexicans reacted quickly and began firing. Robinson was the first man to die in the attack. The Texans waited until daybreak to fire at the fort. They could not waste ammunition. Every shot had to count. The Texans almost halted the Mexicans' firing as soldier after soldier fell under the Texans' fire. A heavy rain began to fall. The Texans took advantage of the downpour and raced for the ship.

From the ship, they could hit any man who came to fire the Mexican cannon. Colonel Francisco Ugartechea, commander of the fort, climbed to the cannon. He was a brave man. The Texans liked him. They cheered him before they began firing again.

Ugartechea waved a white flag. He surrendered. His losses had been too great. He agreed to retreat with what was left of his garrison to below the Rio Grande.

The cannon was not used at Anahuac. By the time the schooner had docked, Travis and Jack had been released. Some of the colonists had gone for Colonel José de las Piedras, senior officer in charge at Nacogdoches. They had told him of the injustices of Bradburn's rule. They had warned him of an immediate battle if something were not done quickly.

Piedras moved to the garrison at Anahuac. He listened to the complaints. He freed Travis and Jack. He ordered Bradburn back to Mexico. The colonists had tarred and feathered men before. Bradburn, afraid of the same treatment, slipped away in the night.

Although the fighting had taken place at Velasco, the first Texas rebellion was called the Battle of Anahuac. It died as quickly as it had flamed. Those who took part were not punished by the Mexican government.

Anahuac settled once again into a peaceful settlement. Travis was well-respected for his actions in defying Bradburn's rules. He and his friends often entertained others with their tales of how they had tricked Bradburn.

While everything on the surface appeared peaceful, the seed of dissatisfaction with the Mexican government had been planted. It would take root quickly and grow rapidly. Perhaps Travis sensed this. His practical pranks seem to have ended with Bradburn's departure. He became more intense about the plight of all Texans.

IV

THE POLITICIAN

Travis was a farsighted young man. He wanted Texas to be a free state. The Mexicans had promised the Texans their own government when the population was great enough to warrant it. Travis saw too many things that the Mexican government had promised and did not carry through.

Although he respected Stephen F. Austin, the empresario for the colonies, Travis felt the quiet, methodical man acted too slowly. Two political parties were established among the colonists. The peace party was led by Austin. Austin urged patience and caution. He wanted the colonists to remain neutral. Travis was one of the leaders of the war party. The war party was convinced that a full rebellion against Mexican rule was the only solution to their problems.

Travis had been in Texas for over a year. He was young, quick tempered, and felt he had a lot of living to do. He wanted to make a fortune. He saw a new state as a new political career along with his law practice. He was totally committed to his new country.

Not too long after the Battle of Anahuac, he decided that it was time to move on. He packed his meager possessions and moved to San Felipe de Austin, the unofficial capital of the American settlements. He felt that San Felipe was where decisions regarding the Texans would be made. He wanted to be a part of those decisions. He wanted to establish himself permanently in the changing country.

San Felipe was an exciting town. It had a stimulating atmosphere for Travis. His friends Patrick Jack and "Three-Legged Willie" Williamson were also residents. Jack joined his brother's law practice. Williamson had his own office.

The town was bustling with activity. It was made up of four plazas or squares. The center two plazas were called the Constitution Plaza and the Military Plaza. The Constitution Plaza housed the church, the rectory, and various places of business. The community barracks, the arsenal, and Camp Santo Cemetery made up Military Plaza.

On most days, people had to walk around the stock grazing in the plazas. All citizens had free grazing rights to public domain land. No one paid any attention to the wandering stock. The stock farmer's only responsibility was to brand his stock. Horses, mules, cattle, hogs, sheep, and goats were raised at almost no expense to the stockmen.

There were some thirty or so houses made of unhewn logs with clapboard roofs. Three or four stores, two blacksmith shops, three hotels, two or three taverns, a town hall, a printing plant, and a hospital were intermingled throughout the plazas.

San Felipe was the cultural and economic center of the colony as well as the seat of government. It offered many advantages to Travis that he did not have in Anahuac. Travis was a regular customer at an elegant store owned by Alexander Somerville. The store specialized in luxurious materials. Travis frequently purchased materials for shirts: "six yards of domestic at thirty-one and one-fourth cents" along with thread and linen. He bought "one pair of suspenders at thirty-seven and one-half cents, one pair of stockings at $1.00, and one vest."

Mrs. Huff, a seamstress, made Travis' shirts for him. He went to a tailor for pantaloons and coats. His white hats were bought from Lewis L. Veeder, who sold wool hats made by the famous hatter William B. Bridges. The hats were guaranteed rain proof.

Travis himself practiced moderation in drink. However, he was pleased to find an abundant supply of whiskey in San Felipe. He often gave whiskey for gifts. He enjoyed arranging social affairs. He furnished the drink as well as paid the fiddler with a small amount of money and so many drinks. Sometimes he gave his host a bottle of liquor for the use of his house.

The hotels in San Felipe were well run. They catered to their guests' wishes. Stables and stablemen were provided for the comfort of the guests' mounts and teams. Boarders were accepted by the day or by the month. One hotel had a tailor who "cleaned and repaired coats, pantaloons, etc., in the best style and on the shortest notice."

Travis boarded at Peyton's hotel. His friend "Three-Legged Willie" lived there. The hotel had the reputation for having the best cook in the community. The Peytons' small daughter, Mag, was the pet of all who stayed there. Travis often played with Mag. He liked children. Mag loved the small gifts he brought her. She was for a time a substitute for his son, left behind in Alabama. Travis missed Charles Edward.

Travis thrived in the business community. He wrote wills, recovered stolen goods and returned them to their rightful owners. He fought the sale of a blind horse and won. He took on any job for a fee. And he accepted anything and everything for the fee.

When he felt his legal practice had been firmly

established, he moved just outside San Felipe. The log structure was a combination living quarters and office. The house had two rooms with a covered open space between the rooms. The empty space was called the dogtrot. Each room had its own fireplace. Travis used one room for his bedroom and across the dogtrot the second room became his library office. He took his meals at the boarding house so he had no need for a kitchen.

San Felipe attracted people from everywhere. Some came and stayed. Others came and drifted away. But Travis mingled with men of action. He was in the middle of history-making events.

On October 31, 1832, fifty representatives from the Texas colonies held a meeting in San Felipe. Travis was in the group. Stephen F. Austin was elected president of the convention. He was not in favor of rebellion. He wanted the colonists to act under the Mexican law.

The colonists were angry at the Mexican government. The group wrote a list of reforms with which to petition the Mexican government. They wanted Texas to be separated from Coahuila. They asked that the law prohibiting immigration to Texas be repealed. They requested an extension of tariff exemptions. They needed an improvement of the judicial system which governed them.

Two men were chosen to carry the petition to Mexico. Austin wanted reform under the Mexican rule. He warned them to be calm. The Mexican officials at Bexar discouraged them from going to Mexico with the petition. The group did not present the petition. But the meeting was proof to all Texans that the war party was active. They would no longer sit calmly in the face of Mexican injustices.

Austin went on a tour of the colonies to calm them after the convention failed. During his absence from San Felipe, another convention was called. On April 1, 1833, new leadership took over. Sam Houston, a newcomer to Texas, was chosen as chairman of the committee to adopt a state constitution.

Travis watched Sam Houston. He remembered the tales of his childhood when Houston fought in the Creek war. Sam was big and handsome. He was a man of action. Travis was pleased that they were both in the war party.

The group, under Houston's leadership, wrote the state constitution. They were smart enough to know that Austin was the man to present it to the Mexican government. Austin knew the language and he was respected by the Mexican officials. He was asked by the convention to deliver and present the document. Austin accepted. What the convention did not realize was that with Austin absent, there was no central leadership. Both the war party and the peace party became increasingly active.

Travis did not dwell on the problems of the Texans. He reacted when he felt the need. Between those times he was busy with his private life. He was highly respected by the community of San Felipe as well as those he had met at the conventions.

The first two years at San Felipe, he practiced law independently. By 1834, his business had increased so much that he had to hire a clerk. He began handling more important cases for which he was paid high fees.

His friend "Three-Legged Willie" Williamson referred many law cases to him. Travis had campaigned for and helped Willie to win the election for the alcalde (mayor) of San Felipe in 1833. The alcalde was also the judge. He was not partial to his friends when they tried a case before him. He fined Travis five dollars one time for contempt of court.

On one occasion Travis, Patrick Jack, and Williamson had to travel to Stafford's Point for a trial. Travis represented a man accused of branding his neighbor's yearlings. Jack represented the neighbor, the plaintiff. David G. Burnet presided over the court which was held under the live oak trees a short distance from the Rose house.

Travis lost the case. He gave notice of appeal and Judge Burnet granted a second trial. The judge also called a recess until after lunch. The case had attracted other lawyers, alcaldes, and ranchers. Dr. Pleasant W. Rose turned over to them a clearing near his house where they could all camp out. While they all sat around their noon meal, the case resolved itself. One of the neighboring ranchmen bought the cattle in question and charges were dropped.

Since the trial had attracted so many people, they decided to have a "frolic," a dance. Mrs. Rose, a religious woman, had not heard preaching for over a year. She asked everyone to attend a service instead of a frolic. A Mr. Woodruff was asked to preach. He had no Bible from which to read a scripture. He led in prayer and the singing of hymns. Travis promised Mrs. Rose a Bible if he could find one in San Felipe.

Travis could find no Bible in San Felipe. He wrote a note of apology to Mrs. Rose. He sent the two Rose daughters a Sunday school book. He was concerned for the religious community in Texas. He remained a Methodist although he had to swear that he was Catholic to own land. In the fall of 1835, he wrote to newspapers in the East of the need "for a few preachers to come to this new land to dispense the tidings of salvation to upwards of 60,000 of destitute souls."

The concern for a religious community did not keep him from enjoying a varied life. He entertained lavishly. He loved "frolics." And he loved beautiful women. He courted many Anglo and Mexican women. He gambled, although he lost more often than he won. He continued to read one literary classic after another. He read everything he could find by Sir Walter Scott, his idol.

In many ways Travis was as romantic as Scott. Like Scott's writing, he was imaginative, unrealistic, and impractical. He was sentimental and emotional. He idealized the Texas situation. He saw the beauty of being a free state with its own government. He did not acknowledge the horror of the war that would pay for that freedom.

On one hand he was a hard lawyer. On the other hand he was very generous. He often charged exorbitant fees for his services. Yet, he thought nothing of buying a friend a pair of shoes. He paid friends' rent, lent clothes, guns, and even his horse. One time he paid the expenses for a neighbor's funeral.

In late 1833, Travis met Miss Rebecca Cummings. At the time he thought he was in love with a Miss E. Henrie. He escorted Rebecca to parties hoping to make "Miss E." jealous. He had two rivals for her affection. When "Miss E." married A. C. Westfall on December 31, 1833, Travis attended the wedding. He also loaned "Shirt and drawers" to the groom to wear to the ceremony.

Travis wasn't heartbroken. He still had the affection of the beautiful Rebecca Cummings. Rebecca lived at Mill Creek, seven miles from San Felipe. She lived with her brother John who operated an inn.

Travis met Rebecca in early fall of 1833. He had stopped at the picturesque inn for a meal. Rebecca helped her bachelor brother to run the inn. Rebecca, thirty years old and beautiful, attracted Travis' attention. By the beginning of 1834, Travis was pursuing her with "schoolboy ardor."

By February he was exchanging notes with her. He made frequent trips to Mill Creek. On March 9th, he wrote in his diary: "Started to Mill Creek, waters swimming and prairie so boggy — could not go — THE FIRST TIME I EVER TURNED BACK IN MY LIFE —."

And it was possibly the only time Travis ever turned back. He was not a man to give up easily. While he was courting Rebecca, he was trying to get custody of his son, Charles Edward. After Travis left Alabama, Susan Isabella was born. He and Rosanna had agreed that the father could have the son and the mother could have the daughter. For some reason Rosanna did not fulfill the agreement. Twice Travis thought Charles Edward was on his way to Texas. And twice he was disappointed.

He could not marry Rebecca because he was still married to Rosanna. He and Rebecca often quarreled. Travis sent or took small gifts and talked her out of being angry.

They took long walks together. They rode horses and picnicked on the prairie. Rebecca gave Travis a lock of her hair which meant that she was very serious about him. The trips to Mill Creek became more frequent for Travis.

John Cummings, Rebecca's brother, became concerned about the future of his sister. He liked Buck Travis but there was too much gossip. He didn't want his sister to be hurt. Their parents were dead so he was responsible for her well-being. He insisted on talking to Travis about his intentions. Buck was younger than Rebecca and he just might not be serious.

Travis explained that his wife would not divorce him. He told John about trying to get his son. He was afraid to do anything about a divorce until his son got to Texas. Travis convinced John that he loved Rebecca.

Rebecca was willing to wait for Travis to be free. He gave her a broach. She gave him a ring to seal their agreement. The ring was made of hammered gold with a black cat's eye stone. When Rebecca gave the ring to Travis, she did not realize how many people would see the ring that reminded them of the love between Rebecca Cummings and William Barret Travis.

The ring, as dramatic as the man to whom it was given, now holds an honored place in the Alamo.

V

THE REBEL

Travis seemed to have unbounded energy. While he was courting Rebecca, he was also furthering his political career. On February 5, 1834, he was appointed secretary of the town council. He was pleased to be recognized as a public official. "Three-Legged Willie" was the alcalde. The two men were a political team for the war party.

They were in a good position of leadership. The colonists had just received word that Stephen F. Austin had been imprisoned in Mexico. Leadership was needed to quieten the settlers. Austin asked that the colonists sit quietly. If they reacted against the Mexican government, his position would be worsened. He still felt that the Texans could work out their problems under the Mexican rule.

Travis used his writing ability to plead for the release of Austin. He first distributed the petition as a handbill in the colonies. In July it was published by the *Texas Republican.* The petition was similar to a plea in a criminal court. He urged the Mexican government to realize that Austin was only speaking as a delegate of Texas. The document he carried to Mexico was not an expression of Austin's own feelings. He defended Austin by stating: "If any wrong has been committed it has not been by Colonel Austin — If any treason has been intended the whole people of Texas alone are guilty."

Travis respected Austin but he disagreed with

him. He believed open rebellion against Mexico was the only way. But he honored Austin's wish that the Texans remain calm and neutral.

His term as secretary of the town council expired at the end of 1834. He doubled his efforts to enlarge his law practice. He took on a new partner to help with his cases. During the first half of 1835, he tried to remain politically silent in order not to "prejudice the situation of Colonel Austin in Mexico."

Travis hoped the colonists would understand their rights and assert themselves. The peace party was in control and leadership was badly needed.

Personal problems took much of Travis' time and energy during this time. He had filed an application for a land grant in Austin's colony in 1831. The land had not been granted. In April, 1835, he was granted a headright in Milam's colony. He received the league of land in payment for legal work.

Unexpectedly in November, Rosanna showed up in San Felipe with both children. Charles Edward was six. He no longer knew his father. Isabella was four. She had never seen Travis. Rosanna wanted to stay as Travis' wife. He no longer loved her. She demanded that they live together as a family or she was going to leave.

Rosanna returned to Alabama with a statement signed by Travis that would enable her to get a divorce. Charles Edward remained in Texas. Travis boarded his son with Mr. and Mrs. David Ayers of Montville near Washington-on-the-Brazos. Charles Edward attended Miss Lydia McHenry's school. The children of the Ayers and surrounding neighbors attended the privately run school as there were no public schools.

Charles Edward was happy with the Ayers.

Travis visited his son as often as possible. They fished together. The father sometimes read to his son. He gave Charles Edward money to buy molasses for Mrs. Ayers to make cookies. They had a good father and son relationship.

Travis did not talk to the small boy about the problems in his new home. Charles Edward was too young to understand. He dreamed of great things for his son. There were times when he watched Charles Edward play that he wondered if he had been wise in keeping him in Texas. Travis could feel war coming.

Santa Anna, president of Mexico, was exercising his power over Texas. He was more hostile than ever. He reopened the custom houses at Anahuac. He charged the colonists duties. Captain Antonio Tenorio was sent to Anahuac to make the colonists pay. Along the coast Mexican garrisons began to concentrate on stopping smuggling and collecting custom duties. The Mexicans captured the Texas schooner *Martha.* The schooner was loaded with supplies for the colonists. The colonists took a note from a messenger that hinted that more troops were on the way.

The colonists were angry. They burned some lumber that Tenorio had ordered at Anahuac. Without thinking of the consequences, Travis reacted dramatically. He quickly raised a troop of twenty-five men from the war party and marched on Tenorio's headquarters. He gave the Mexicans fifteen minutes to surrender or to be "put to the sword."

Tenorio asked Travis to let him consider it overnight. Travis refused. The Mexicans surrendered sixty-four muskets and bayonets and twenty-one cartridge boxes. Travis divided them among his men. He allowed Tenorio and his men to keep twelve muskets to protect them against Indians when they reached the interior.

The Mexican soldiers and their leaders were boarded on the *Ohio*, a ship that carried them to Harrisburg. At Harrisburg the colonists were having a Fourth of July celebration. Tenorio and his men joined in the party. Tenorio attended a ball that night as guest of the Americans.

The next morning, Travis made sure the Mexicans were on their way toward La Bahia. He returned to San Felipe very pleased with himself. The colonists were not so pleased with him.

The colonists had supported his fight with Bradburn. But this was more than the results of practical pranks. The peace party saw this as an act of open rebellion. He had thrown out the garrison commander.

Travis apologized in the wake of criticism. He wrote to Henry Smith, "This act has been done with the most patriotic motives. I hope you and my fellow citizens generally will approve it, or excuse it." He wrote to Jim Bowie that "the *peace-party* . . . are the strongest. . . . Unless we could be united, had we not better be quiet, and settle down for a while? . . . I am determined, for one, to go with my countrymen; right or wrong, 'sink or swim, live or die, survive or perish,' I am with them!"

He put aside his prejudice against Mexican authority to write to Colonel Domingo de Ugartechea, military commandant of Coahuila-Texas. He offered to correspond with Ugartechea in order "to lend my feeble aid to any plan which may be called on to bring about happy and peaceful termination" to their problems. "Their only want is a good understanding between the government and the people of Texas to set things right."

Santa Anna, the "Napoleon of the West," took Travis' apology as a sign of weakness. He decided this was the time to put a stop to the Texas uprising. He told General Martin Perfecto de Cós, his brother-in-law, to take personal command of the troops in Texas.

Cós' first action was to order the arrest of Travis, "Three-Legged Willie," and some other prominent citizens. Not only were they to be arrested, but their own officials were ordered to make the arrests. It was one thing for the colonists to criticize their own men. It was quite another thing for them to turn them over to the Mexicans for trial.

The peace party had supported Santa Anna. Now they turned against him overnight. They were shocked into recognizing Santa Anna's acts toward martial law and military occupation of Texas. Committees of Safety sprang up in every town. Public opinion changed. Travis was excused for his actions at Anahuac.

He expressed the feelings of the Texans as well as his own when he wrote to his friend John W. Moore, ". . . The devil has shown his cloven foot, and his lies will be believed no longer. . . . A tremendous reaction has taken place, . . . The word now is, a convention of all Texas, to declare our sentiments, and to prepare for defense, if necessary. . . . God grant that all Texas men stand . . . in the 'hour that will try men's souls.' "

Travis, Moseley Baker, and four others traveled over Texas to inform them and to encourage them into action. The Mexicans were worried about the success of the group. Cós ordered them arrested.

Again the colonists refused. Travis felt the trip was successful. He wrote to his friend John Moore on August 24, 1835, "The whole upper country are unanimously for a convention in which the voice of the people will be freely expressed."

Stephen F. Austin returned from his imprisonment in Mexico on September 1, 1835. He found the colonists in a state of fear and confusion. A banquet was planned for September 8th at Brazoria to celebrate his return. Close to 1,000 people crammed the banquet hall to honor Austin. They wanted to know how their leader felt after almost two years in a Mexican prison.

Much to Travis' pleasure, Austin left little doubt about his feelings. He now was in accord with the war party. He no longer believed that Texas could become a free state under Mexican rule. "War," Austin said, "is our only resource. There is no other remedy but to defend our rights, ourselves, and our country by force of arms."

A convention was now a necessity. Travis turned his attention to the election of delegates. He wrote to friends of political standing to support certain persons of the war party. It was as if he had taken on the cause of Texas freedom single-handed.

Austin recognized Travis' ability for leadership. At the time of Travis' early pranks, Austin disapproved of his rash actions. Now he realized that Travis had been farsighted in seeing the war. The work of Travis and the war party was bearing fruit. Members of the war party had gone to New Orleans to seek help. They returned with five cannons, one hundred kegs of powder, and some lead and shot.

On September 21st, Austin issued a command to arm. He hoped for two forces. One would be immediately active. The second would be on reserve. Every man was to supply himself with food and arms. Travis joined the Federal Army of Texas as a lieutenant in Captain Randall Jones' Company on September 28th.

The forces that gathered at the end of September were to stop Cós. He was headed toward San Antonio de Bexar with 400 soldiers. Captain Randall Jones' Company was to keep him in the lower country.

The Mexican forces were aware of the Texans' strategy. They had to distract the attention from Cós. The colonists at Gonzales had a cannon. The Mexicans decided to take it. The Texans hid the cannon and sent out a cry for help. Volunteers rushed to the scene. On October 2nd, the Mexicans were defeated. While the Gonzales battle got attention, Cós slipped into the Alamo and took control of Bexar.

Travis missed the first battle of the Revolution. He wrote to Captain Jones to explain his absence, "... I have been quite sick with influenza or I should have gone — I expect to go in a few days. ..."

He seemed more interested at that time with the proposed convention than with war skirmishes. His soliciting of votes for delegates paid off. When the election returns came in, he and six of his closest friends were chosen. They were all staunch members of the war party.

The convention was set for October 15th. On October 16th, one day after the date set, only thirty official delegates from the eighty chosen could be found. Austin had been called to Gonzales.

Much confusion kept the camp in a state of disorder. A vote was called. Austin was elected commander-in-chief of the Texas army. He was determined to shape the volunteers into something of an army. By the middle of October, he was on his way to recapture the Alamo. He asked that all who could, come to Gonzales prepared to fight.

Travis forgot about the convention and responded to the call. He was at the council of war on the 19th of October. The council decided to go to Salado, five miles east of San Antonio de Bexar. They were to wait for reinforcements and observe enemy movement. Travis was in the group that marched toward Bexar.

Sam Houston arrived from Nacogdoches. He disapproved of Austin's plans. He encouraged the delegates to leave the ranks and return to San Felipe for the convention. He cautioned the Texans that they were ill-equipped against the trained Mexican army.

Austin asked the army to vote on whether the delegates should return and hold the convention. The vote was in favor of dismissing those delegates who wanted to return. Travis, who had worked so hard for the convention, chose to remain with the army.

Jim Bowie and James Fannin made camp at Concepción Mission. Travis was put in charge of a volunteer company of cavalry soldiers. He was pleased with his assignment. The cavalry unit had to be excellent horsemen and fast. Travis hand-picked the men under his command.

The promotion was a compliment to Travis. The principal duty of the cavalry was to scout the movements of the Mexican army. The assignments were risky. The commander needed speed of movement and to be quick thinking. Travis felt that he was perfectly suited for the job.

The cavalry moved from place to place. They scouted the enemy and reported to Austin. Grass was burned to prevent the Mexican soldiers from using it to graze their horses. Mexican horses were captured for the Texas army.

Travis became unhappy with his command. Nothing was really happening. In November he tried to resign his post. Confusion was spreading among the Texas troops. Many of the men were leaving to return to their homes. Austin needed Travis' support. He did not accept his resignation. He did write a commendation for Travis to present to the Consultation.

The Consultation was still gathered at San Felipe. They discouraged outright war. The Texans did not have the supplies nor the men. Austin, along with W. H. Wharton and Dr. Branch T. Archer, was appointed to go to the United States to ask for funds to finance the Texas war.

Austin gave a command for the Texas troops to capture Bexar. Sam Houston did not agree. The Texas ranks were divided. Travis agreed with Austin but he did not command enough men to storm the town.

Discouraged by the lack of support, Austin turned his command over to Colonel Edward Burleson. He returned to San Felipe to prepare for his trip to the United States. Travis, equally discouraged, went to Mill Creek to visit Rebecca Cummings.

It was while he was there that he learned of his new appointment. A provisional government had been set up by the Consultation. A military body was appointed. Sam Houston was appointed major-general and commander of the regular army. Colonel James Fannin was colonel of the artillery. Under Fannin's command, Travis was promoted to first major.

When he learned of the appointment, he immediately resigned. He supported Francis W. Johnson as his replacement. The resignation was accepted. Johnson filled the position.

Travis had not given up his loyalty to Texas as a free state. He wrote a detailed recommendation for the structure of a strong military body. Both Austin and Houston approved his recommendations. The report was presented to the military committee of the new provisional government.

The military committee approved the report. A few changes were made in the number and kinds of arms for the soldiers. Travis was pleased when the cavalry was unanimously approved. He felt the cavalry was "indispensible to the services of Texas during the present struggle." He recommended that "the cavalry should be commanded by a Lt. Col. who should be subject alone to the orders of the commander in chief." On Christmas Eve, 1835, Travis was commissioned lieutenant colonel of the Texas army. It was the appointment he wanted. It appealed to the romantic side of the young man who had grown up with legends of great heroes. He envisioned himself astride a great mount in full uniform.

The cavalry was the only military unit for which a uniform had been prescribed. It was to be "a suit of cadet gray cloth coats, yellow bullet buttons, and pantaloons for winter, and two suits of gray cottonade roundabouts, and pantaloons for summer, and fur caps, black cloth stocks and cowhide boots."

Travis was excited as he stood for his tailor to measure him for a winter uniform. Just as he had dreamed as a boy of "Swamp Fox," he now dreamed of great things. His imaginative, romantic, youthful mind relieved the tensions of the past months. The deep lines of worry and anxiety were gone from his handsome face when he said to himself, "Just wait until Rebecca sees me in full regalia!"

VI

"VICTORY OR DEATH!"

Rebecca Cummings would never see Travis in his uniform. The uniform was soon forgotten with the turn of events.

Ben Milam had led an attack on Cós the first week in December. It had been a strange battle. Cós was in the Alamo. His troops were scattered over the town as well as in the mission. The Texans had him surrounded but no one would do anything.

Burleson, who had taken Austin's command, wanted to leave the area. Milam disagreed. When Milam yelled, "Who will come with Old Ben Milam?" more than 300 men joined him.

Milam was one of the first Texans to be killed in the battle. For four days the men fought from house to house. The Mexican soldiers were baffled. They had never seen a battle like this. The Texans fought like they were on an animal hunt. There was no strategy to the fight. Each man was concerned with his own survival. Cós surrendered. On December 10th, Cós agreed to leave Bexar and not return.

Many of the Texans believed the war was over. Travis and Austin did not. Many of the volunteers left for home. Colonel Frank Johnson went to get permission from the provisional governor to take the port of Matamoros. Johnson left Colonel James C. Neill in command at Bexar. Dr. James Grant did not wait for Johnson's return. On December 30th, he took two hundred volunteers with him to go to Matamoros. The men looted the town before they left. They took everything of value, money, clothing, saddles, arms, food, blankets, and medical supplies.

On January 6, 1836, Colonel Neill wrote to the authorities in San Felipe: "It will be appalling to you to learn and see herewith our alarming weakness." He had only 104 men. There was no food or clothing. Most of the men had only one shirt and one blanket. "If there has ever been a dollar here, I have no knowledge of it."

Neill thought conditions could not get worse. But they did. The men were to have received their October pay. Nothing came. More men left the ranks. Neill knew he could not hold the town and the mission with so few men. He ordered his men to the Alamo. Green B. Jameson wrote to Sam Houston, "You can plainly see that the Alamo never was built by a military people as a fortress."

General Sam Houston established headquarters of the army at Washington-on-the-Brazos. He placed troops and provisions at strategic points. He asked for the appointment of "the field-officers proper to command and superintend the several recuriting stations."

Colonel William Barret Travis, of the first regiment of infantry, was ordered to the recruiting station at San Felipe. On January 9th, Houston went to Goliad to organize troops under James Walker Fannin's command. Rumors were flying that Santa Anna, angered at Cós' surrender, was on his way to Bexar. Few people believed the stories. Santa Anna would not come in midwinter when there was no grass for his horses.

Travis, along with other recruiting officers, complained of lack of funds. Travis worked hard to recruit volunteers. He had planned to join the Matamoros expedition, but the plans had fallen through. The expedition only created more problems. It was disastrous from the start.

Houston forwarded Neill's letter of January 6th to Travis. Houston ordered Jim Bowie to take a detachment of thirty men to Bexar. They were to dismantle the Alamo and abandon the fort. He wrote to Governor Smith of his actions. Before Governor Smith received Houston's letter, he ordered Travis to take a force of 100 men to relieve Neill at Bexar.

Bowie arrived in Bexar before Travis. He decided to disobey Houston's orders. Neill and he agreed that Bexar was the stronghold of Texas. Bowie set about repairing and setting up defense against the Mexican troops. He used his friendship with the Mexicans. He had been a part of the community when he lived in the city with his beautiful wife Ursula. They remembered how heartbroken Bowie had been when his family had died in the cholera epidemic.

The Mexicans relayed messages to him about the movement of the Mexican army. With the aid of his friends, Bowie got horses for scouting. Forty head of cattle were brought to him. One hundred bushels of corn and ammunition for the eighteen-pounder were stored in the mission. The Alamo began to take on the appearance of a real fort. The spirits of the men were lifted. A rally was held. Jim Bowie and James Bonham, who had come to Texas to join his childhood friend Buck Travis, were the first ones to sign the resolution to hold the fort.

On February 2nd, they learned that thousands of Mexicans were marching toward Bexar. The situation was critical. Bowie wrote to Governor Smith,

"Our force is very small, the returns of this day to the Comdt. is only one hundred and twenty officers and men. It would be a waste of men to put our brave little band against thousands."

In many ways, things were almost as bad in San Felipe. The council had impeached Governor Smith. Governor Smith had fired the council. They were so involved with their own struggles of power that they had lost sight of the poor conditions of their army. Houston had become impatient with the fighting at San Felipe. He went to East Texas to work out a treaty with the Indians who were threatening to join the Mexicans against the Texans. Funds that had been raised for provisions for the army were used for other things.

When Travis received his orders to go to Bexar, he reacted quickly. He asked for money, provisions, and clothing and an additional 500 men. His requests were sensible. They simply were not fulfilled.

Travis had thirty-nine men. He spent over one hundred dollars of his own money for supplies. He bought "flour, tin ware, twine leggins and spurs, flag and powder flask, a bridle, blankets, a tent, frying pan, and rope." His second order of supplies added corn, coffee, sugar, and additional blankets for his men. He also advanced "seventeen dollars in bounty to his men."

On January 23rd he set out for Bexar. He was not pleased with what he had been able to do. He had envisioned the command of a great force marching to Bexar. He was in charge of a small group that should have been commanded by an officer of lesser rank.

He camped on the Colorado to dispatch a message to Governor Smith. Nine of his men had deserted. They had taken the provisions that he had supplied them. Two of the men had taken good horses and equipment which Travis had helped to buy. Travis became so depressed he resigned his post.

Governor Smith ignored the resignation. After several days of waiting for a reply to his letter, Travis marched on toward Bexar. The small reinforcement led by Travis reached Bexar on February 3rd. The thirty men of his group brought the total forces up to 150 men.

Travis did not have time to brood. Bowie and Neill had "come to the solemn resolution that we will rather die in these ditches than give it up to the enemy." Travis began to work as hard as the other men to strengthen the fort.

On January 9th, their attention was drawn to the arrival of a group of "Tennessee boys." Colonel David Crockett arrived with the Tennessee Mounted Volunteers. Everyone stopped what they were doing. Davy Crockett was a born entertainer. Everyone gathered in the Main Plaza to hear him speak. The legendary Davy Crockett had come to take up Texas' fight for freedom as his own.

Although Crockett added only a dozen or so men to the group of defenders, spirits soared. On the day after his arrival, a great party, a fandango, was held for Crockett. Bexar was noted for its beautiful women. They worked hard. They played with equal enthusiasm.

The fandango was a welcome relief from the hard work of preparing the fort. The men danced and flirted with beautiful women. They told tall tales, each trying to outdo the other. The party had reached a peak of dancing, talk, and laughter when a messenger arrived at one o'clock.

The messenger was covered with dust. His horse was covered with foamy sweat. He insisted on seeing Colonel Erasmo Seguin. Seguin was not present. Travis was senior officer in Bexar. The messenger gave the letter to him. Palacio Benavides had written, "At this moment I have received a very certain notice that the commander-in-chief, Antonio Lopéz de Santa Anna, marches for the city of San Antonio to take possession thereof with 16,000 men."

Travis read the message and passed it on to Bowie and Crockett. They discussed the marching troops. They figured it would take the troops at least fourteen to fifteen days to reach Bexar. There was no immediate danger. The party continued until seven o'clock the next morning.

Colonel Neill had not been consulted when the messenger arrived. The next day Neill left for home. the reason was family illness. He appointed Travis commander of the Alamo men.

The act caused a crisis. The volunteers who were at the Alamo before Travis arrived were particularly unhappy. Travis had been there only a week. He was too young. Bowie was older and more experienced. He was the one who had put the fort on its feet.

Neill was forced to put the command to a vote. Bowie was elected as "a full colonel in command of the volunteers." That made Bowie a higher rank than Travis. Travis' ego was hurt. He was still in command of the regulars and the cavalry. He was in an awkward position.

Travis appealed to Governor Smith for help, "I feel myself delicately and awkwardly situated — I therefore hope that your Excelly. will give me some definite orders, . . ." Smith did not respond quickly enough.

Travis and Bowie both agreed that the Alamo was the most important stronghold of Texas. It was far more important to get reinforcements than to argue over the command of the small group they had. On February 14th, they came to an agreement. They would have separate commands. Bowie commanded the volunteers. Travis commanded the regulars and calvary. They agreed to confer on all major actions. They wrote Governor Smith of the agreement and informed him that "All general orders, and correspondence, will hence forth be signed by both."

With the conflict between the men resolved, the morale of the men began to improve. They still did not have enough money or food but excitement of their commitment took hold. They worked with new enthusiasm at fortifying the garrison. Wells for a water supply were dug. Walls were mended. Ammunition was gathered and stored.

The men developed a new respect for Travis. He worked constantly at his post. His concern for the welfare of the men won him new loyalties. His requests for reinforcements strengthened their convictions to hold Bexar.

Travis did not believe that Santa Anna could reach Bexar before the middle or late March. He did not want to take any chances. On February 16, he sent his best horseman and friend, Jim Bonham, to Goliad with a message to Fannin to bring his 420 men immediately.

For several days rumors were brought to Travis about the approaching Mexican army. There was no doubt in his mind that the army was coming. He just didn't believe that it was coming so quickly. On February 20th, he received a message that he could not explain away.

Captain Juan Seguin served in a company of local Mexicans. They supported the Texan cause. Seguin came from an influential family. He knew the country well. He hand-picked his scouts. He had absolute trust in his cousin Blas Herrera. He had sent Herrera to Laredo to watch for enemy movement. Herrera had returned with startling news. Seguin sent for Travis.

Travis was surprised when Herrera told him that he had seen the Mexicans crossing the Rio Grande. Santa Anna had arrived in Texas!

Travis called a war council at nine o'clock that night. He asked Blas Herrera to repeat his story. The Texans argued for hours whether to believe him. Travis chose to ignore the warning. He just did not believe that Santa Anna could move his troops so rapidly.

At sunup on February 23rd, the narrow streets of Bexar were bustling with activity. Travis watched with frustration. The citizens were evacuating the town. He could not learn why. Each one questioned gave him the same answer. They were moving to begin farming.

Around eleven o'clock a friendly Mexican informed Travis that Santa Anna was within eight miles of Bexar. Santa Anna had planned a surprise attack on the 22nd. He had been held up by a norther and heavy rains. Now he was on the move. The local citizens had been warned to move from the town.

Travis and Dr. John Sutherland climbed the winding stairs to the belfry of San Fernando Cathedral. They could see nothing. A sentry was left to watch. He was instructed to ring the bell if he saw the Mexicans.

Travis had not reached his post before the sentry rang the bell. He had seen the sun glance off the swords of the soldiers. People climbed on the rooftop of the church. They could see nothing. They reprimanded the sentry. He tried to explain that he had seen them. The soldiers were hiding behind bushes.

Travis saw nothing, but he did not want to take chances. He called for volunteers to scout the area. Dr. John Sutherland and John W. Smith volunteered. They worked out a simple signal. If they turned their horses to return to Bexar in a run, they had sighted the army. The sentry was to ring the bell at once.

At the crest of a hill about two miles from town, the scouts saw the Mexicans. A well-mounted and well-equipped Mexican vanguard was only a hundred and fifty yards away. Sutherland and Smith stayed only long enough to guess at the number of soldiers. There were between twelve and fifteen hundred men.

The sentry rang the bell as soon as he saw the scouts dashing toward Bexar. By the time Sutherland and Smith arrived, Travis had ordered his entire force to move inside the Alamo. The Mexican troops arrived by midafternoon.

Travis quickly wrote to Gonzales for help:

> The enemy in large force is in sight. We want men and provisions. Send them to us. We have one hundred and fifty men and are determined to defend the Alamo to the last. Give us assistance.

He still had hopes that Jim Bonham would return soon with good news. He could not wait for an answer. He had taken too many chances already. He decided to send another message to Goliad.

The messengers, Sutherland and Smith, had not

traveled too far when they heard a rider approaching. It was Jim Bonham. Fannin wasn't responding to Travis' call for help. While Bonham was explaining that help was not coming, the men heard a cannon fire.

"Come back with us," Sutherland told Bonham.

"You can't get through," Smith warned him. "It'll be certain death!"

Jim Bonham sat tall on his horse and looked toward the Alamo. A mischievous smile crossed his tired face as he remembered his childhood with Travis. "Buck and I have stuck together too long for me to turn back now. Besides, boys, this looks like it's going to be a good fight."

The messengers rode hard and fast toward their destinations. Bonham turned his horse toward the Alamo.

The shot the men had heard was Travis' answer to Santa Anna's hoisting of a blood-red flag. The red flag meant that no mercy would be shown the Alamo defenders. The firing of the cannon was Travis' way of saying, "You will have to come and get us!"

Bowie was very ill. He could no longer command the volunteers. He turned the command over to Travis early the morning of February 24th. The morning was quiet but by early afternoon firing began. Occasionally the Texans answered fire but mostly they saved their ammunition. It was dark when the Texans could check their losses. No one had been hurt.

Travis used the quiet time to write his message "To The People of Texas & All Americans in The World." The message in part said:

> I am besieged by a thousand or more Mexicans under Santa Anna . . . *I shall never surrender or*

retreat. Then, I call on you in the name of Liberty, of patriotism & everything dear to the American character, to come to our aid with all dispatch . . . If this call is neglected, I am determined to sustain myself as long as possible & die a soldier who never forgets what is due to his own honor & that of his country —

Victory or Death
William Barret Travis
Lt. Col. Comdt.

"Victory or Death," the words which were burned on the caps of "Swamp Fox's" Brigade became Travis' battle cry. Travis chose a special courier, Launcelot Smithers, to deliver the letter.

Smithers was a dedicated follower of Travis. He arrived in San Felipe on Saturday morning, February 27th. At eleven o'clock many leading townspeople held a meeting. Many of Travis' San Felipe friends were present. They drew up resolutions to send aid to the Alamo. Nothing was done. No one went to help him.

The letter did not bring the help Travis needed. It did excite the people. Many couriers were sent to spread the word. All of the communities were informed. Schooners carried the message to other ports. Within five weeks, the whole United States was in an uproar. It was too late.

Travis, unaware that Houston was with the Cherokee Indians, wrote to his commander-in-chief in Gonzales. The morale of the men was high. They had sustained slight injuries but no deaths. Some defenders had been able to slip to surrounding houses and burn them. The enemy now had nothing close to the Alamo behind which to hide. Davy Crockett was keeping the men going with enthusiasm. Travis ended the letter with another plea for help: "If they overpower us, we fall a sacrifice at the shrine of our country, and we hope posterity and our country will do our memory justice. Give me help, oh my country! Victory or death!"

The Alamo was surrounded by the enemy. No one would volunteer to be the courier. The risk was too great. To try to slip past the enemy lines was certain death. It was put to a vote. Juan Seguin was chosen. Travis did not want him to go. Seguin spoke Spanish and understood Mexican customs. They might need him to talk to Santa Anna. The men could not be persuaded. Juan Seguin carried the message to Gonzales.

Seguin took Bowie's horse for the trip. He and his orderly headed toward the Gonzales road. They could not slip past the guards. When the guards called out to them Seguin answered in Spanish that they were friends. Before the guards could stop them, they spurred their horses into action. The guards fired and missed. The fast horses soon outran the pursuing Mexicans.

The cold, miserable days began to wear on the defenders. They had repaired walls, dug trenches, and gathered firewood in the cold northern wind. The Mexican army increased in numbers each day. It seemed as if they were playing a waiting game with the defenders.

On February 27th, Travis wrote another appeal for help. This one went to Fannin at Goliad. Travis chose his most trusted friend, Jim Bonham, to carry the message. If anyone could get through the enemy lines, Jim could. Bonham slipped through the enemy lines in the darkness.

Two days later on the 29th, Travis noticed

strange activities among the Mexican lines. Santa Anna was rearranging his defenses. He had heard that Fannin was on his way with reinforcements for the Alamo. Santa Anna was angry that all of his troops had not arrived. He took men from around the Alamo to guard the roads into Bexar. He left a thin circle of soldiers around the Alamo to keep anyone from leaving.

No one had plans to leave. But a group had plans to enter. Travis' appeal to Gonzales had brought thirty-two volunteers to their aid. At around 3 a.m., Tuesday, March 1st, the Gonzales Ranging Company of Volunteers slipped into the Alamo.

Travis had been very cautious in using ammunition. The arrival of the men from Gonzales called for a celebration. He ordered the twelve-pounder on the west wall to be fired. The double blast was aimed at a house on Main Plaza where the enemy was especially active. One shot missed. The second shot sent stones, timber, and Mexicans flying. The Texans were jubilant. Travis never knew that the celebration shot hit Santa Anna's headquarters.

Rumors reached the defenders that Fannin was coming. Spirits soared. Jim Bonham must have been successful. They expected the forces to arrive no later than March 3rd.

March 3rd arrived with still no sign of help. A little before noon, Travis saw a lone rider in the distance. Jim Bonham had returned. He was alone.

Travis watched Jim's approach to the mission. "What," he asked himself, "have I asked of my friend, except to die for Texas?" He could not give up now. He was totally committed.

Jim's shoulders sagged with weariness and disappointment. His sad eyes reflected his unhappy news. Smiles disappeared on the faces of the expectant defenders when he slightly shook his head from side to side. Before he could dismount, Travis knew that Fannin was not coming.

Travis still believed help would come from San Felipe and surrounding communities. They had made the fort stronger. The morale of the men was kept high by Davy Crockett's fiddle playing and jokes. When they were not exchanging fire with the enemy, they were busy preparing for another siege.

More Mexican soldiers arrived and still no help came for the defenders. Around midnight on March 3rd, Travis decided to send one more messenger through enemy lines. Many of the defenders began writing last notes to send to their families. Travis finished his last official report to be taken to the president of the convention at Washington-on-the-Brazos.

He wrote a personal note which is assumed to have been for Rebecca Cummings. He wrote to his friend Jesse Grimes to deliver the note for him. His last message, written on a sheet of torn yellow wrapping paper, was to David Ayers. Many memories crossed his mind as he thought of his small son. He remembered his last visit with Charles Edward in January before he had left for Bexar.

His note to David Ayers on the torn paper was simple:

> Take care of my little boy. If the country should be saved, I may make him a splendid fortune; but if the country should be lost and I should perish, he will have nothing but the proud recollections that he is the son of a man who died for his country.

Travis gave the messages to John W. Smith. He

told him, "I will fire the eighteen-pounder three times a day—morning, noon, and night—as long as the Alamo stands. When you hear the shots, you will know that I am still fighting."

At dawn on March 4th, the new Mexican battery attacked. It was clear that the Alamo could not take this kind of action very long. By dawn March 5th, the Mexican battery had moved within 200 yards of the Alamo.

In the late afternoon, the Mexican firing stopped abruptly. Travis used the time to call his men together. "Our choice is to surrender, to try and escape, or to stay and fight to the end. There is no longer any real hope of help. I am determined to stay. The choice is yours."

Then legend has spread that Travis drew a line in the dirt and said, "Any man who wants to stay and fight, step across this line." All men, except one, stepped across the line.

Whether there was a line or not, one man, Louis Rose, chose to leave. Bowie and Crockett tried to talk him into staying. Rose did not want to die. To remain was sure death. By dark he had climbed over the wall and slipped downstream in the river.

The night was overcast and dark. Travis decided to use the darkness to get one more message to Fannin. He chose sixteen-year-old Jim Allen to take the message out. Jim had a first-rate horse and was an excellent horseman. The gates flew open and Jim, riding bareback, darted to the open prairie.

Travis walked through the grounds of the Alamo. He went to the chapel where the women and children huddled in fear. He stopped before Mrs. Dickinson, who was holding her fifteen-months-old daughter, Angelina. Travis took his cat's eye stone ring and put a thread of string through it. He gently looped it around Angelina's neck. He then hurried back to the walls.

The garrison was quiet. The men were trying to sleep. Travis was worried. Everything was too quiet. Just at the first streaks of dawn on March 6th, the Mexicans attacked in full force. Captain John Baugh was standing guard on the wall when he heard them coming.

Travis, in his homespun jeans with sword and shotgun, yelled to his men, "Come on, boys! The Mexicans are upon us and we'll give them hell!" Travis remained at the north battery. He shouted again and again, "Hurrah, my boys!"

Twice the Mexicans had to retreat from the walls. The third time they found the weakest section of the wall and came inside the plaza. Travis was on the north wall. He heard ladders hit the wall below him. Before he could fire into the group of men scaling the ladder, a shot rang through the air.

Travis fell. He was hit in the head. His shotgun fell to the enemy. He rolled down the bank of earth against the wall. Stunned and dying his last words were, "Don't surrender, boys!"

Through blood running down his face, Travis saw a Mexican officer coming upon him with a sword. With his last burst of energy, he raised his sword. The two men ran their swords through each other. Both died instantly.

After thirteen days of constant siege, the Alamo fell on March 6, 1836. The 183 defenders took over 600 Mexican soldiers with them in death. The Mexicans were ruthless. They mangled the bodies of the dead Texans.

Santa Anna called for Francisco Ruiz, the

town's alcalde. He wanted positive identification of the leaders at the Alamo. Ruiz identified what was left of the bodies of Travis, Crockett, and Bowie. Santa Anna, pleased with himself, ordered the mangled bodies to be burned.

William Barret Travis, who had lived in the shadow of history-making events, became a national hero overnight. At the early age of twenty-six, he had achieved more than his heroes of the past. He did not have to wait for his memory to become immortal. His words "Victory or Death!" were already imprinted upon the minds of all who had read his message "To The People of Texas & All Americans in The World."

He was young, quick tempered, and quick to act. He was a romantic in his dashing red pantaloons and white hat. He was unrealistic in his belief that so few men could hold the Alamo.

He was heroic in his conviction that the Alamo could save Texas. The words "Victory or death" were burned into the minds of men whose battle cry became "Remember the Alamo" as they fought and *won* Texas' independence.

BIBLIOGRAPHY

Courtesy, Library of the Daughters of Republic of Texas at the Alamo, San Antonio, Texas, "William Barret Travis files and clippings."

Davis, Robert E. *Diary of William Barret Travis: August 30, 1833-June 26, 1834.* Waco: Texian Press, 1966.

Fehrenbach, T. R. *Lone Star: A History of Texas and the Texans.* New York: The Macmillan Company, 1969.

Frantz, Joe B. and others. *Heroes of Texas.* Waco: Texian Press, 1979.

Johnson, William Weber. *The Birth of Texas.* Cambridge: The Riverside Press, 1960.

Lord, Walter. *A Time to Stand.* New York: Harper and Brothers, 1964.

Mixon, Ruby. "William Barret Travis, His Life and Letters." (unpublished thesis for master's degree, The University of Texas at Austin, 1930) Copy at the Library of the Daughters of the Republic of Texas at the Alamo, San Antonio, Texas.

Nevin, David. *The Texans.* New York: Time-Life Books, 1975.

Smithwick, Noah. [Compiled by his daughter Nanna Smithwick Donaldson]. *The Evolution of a State, Recollections of Old Texas Days.* c 1900. [Facsimile by The Steck Company, Austin, Texas, n.d.].

Tinkle, Lon. *The Valiant Few, Crisis at the Alamo.* New York: The Macmillan Company, 1964.

Tolbert, Frank X. *An Informal History of Texas from Cabeza de Vaca to Temple Houston.* New York: Harper and Brothers, 1951.

Turner, Martha Anne. *William Barret Travis, His Sword and His Pen.* Waco: Texian Press, 1972.

Webb, Walter Prescott. [Editor-in-chief]. *The Handbook of Texas,* Vols. I and II. Austin: The Texas State Historical Association, 1952.

Woodman, Jr., David. *Guide to Texas Emigrants.* Waco: Texian Press, 1974.